ICONIC DESIGNS

GREAT
CAR
DESIGNS

1900–TODAY

Richard Spilsbury

D0177287

Raintree is an imprint of Capstone Global Library Limited, a company incorporated in England and Wales having its registered office at 7 Pilgrim Street, London EC4V 6LB – Registered company number: 6695582

www.raintree.co.uk
myorders@raintree.co.uk

Text © Capstone Global Library Limited 2016
The moral rights of the proprietor have been asserted.

Edited by Clare Lewis and Abby Colich
Designed by Richard Parker
Original illustrations © Capstone Global Library 2015
Illustrated by HL Studios
Picture research by Jo Miller
Production by Victoria Fitzgerald
Originated by Capstone Global Library Ltd
Printed and bound in China by Leo Paper Products

ISBN 978 1 406 29670 9 (hardback)
19 18 17 16 15
10 9 8 7 6 5 4 3 2 1

ISBN 978 1 406 29675 4 (paperback)
20 19 18 17 16
10 9 8 7 6 5 4 3 2 1

British Library Cataloguing in Publication Data
A full catalogue record for this book is available from the British Library.

Acknowledgements
We would like to thank the following for permission to reproduce photographs: Alamy: AF archive, 12, Bill Philpot, 22, Heritage Image Partership Ltd/National Motor Museum, 21, Ian Macpherson, 27, Motoring Picture Library, cover, 8, 16, 30, ZUMA Press, Inc, 15; Corbis: Bettmann, 6, Car Culture, 36, Transtock/Johm Lamm, 35; Getty Images: Car Culture, 26, Heritage Images/National Motor Museum, 7, The LIFE Picture Collection/Timepix/Hugo Jaeger, 10; Landov: DPA/ULI DECK, 13, Reuters/Ina Fassbender, 32; Newscom: akg-images/Paul Almasy, 18, ImageBROKER/Martin Mozter, 17, MCT/David M. Warren, 42, NI Syndication, 14, WENN/CB2/ZOB, 39, ZUMA Press/ChinaFotoPress, cover (inset), 43, ZUMA Press/Jean-Francois Galeron, 29, ZUMA Press/Sutton Motorsports, 28; Rex USA: Paul Cooper, 40; Shutterstock: Fedor Selivanov, 24, gallimaufry, 5, Maksim Toome, 23, Natursports, 4; SuperStock: LUCASFILM/20TH CENTURY FOX/Album, 33; Wikimedia, 9, dave_7, 11, Traction.fr, 20

Design Elements
Shutterstock: franco's photos, Jason Winter, URRRA

CONTENTS

Introducing iconic cars 4

Model T Ford 6

Duesenberg J 8

From concept to icon: Volkswagen Beetle 10

The Jeep 14

Mercedes 300SL 16

Citroën DS 18

Designer in focus: Flaminio Bertoni 20

1959 Cadillac 22

The Mini 24

E-type Jaguar 26

Lotus 72 28

Audi Quattro 30

Designer in focus: Martin Smith 32

Toyota Prius 34

From concept to icon: Smart Car 36

Bugatti Veyron 40

The future of car design 42

Timeline 44

Glossary 45

Find out more 46

Index 48

Some words are shown in bold, **like this**. You can find out what they mean by looking in the glossary.

INTRODUCING ICONIC CARS

Imagine a world without cars. Tricky, isn't it? Cars are one of our most convenient forms of transport. They come in an amazing variety of shapes, colours and styles, and all of them are the products of designers.

Car design

Any car design starts with a product **specification**. This is a detailed list of answers to questions such as these:

- What is the car's function, for example, luxury limousine or military SUV?
- What is its form or shape, for example, sleek or boxy shape?
- What materials will it use, for example, plastic, glass or metal?
- How much will it cost?

The design for a racing car needs to be different from a taxi, because they have different functions.

CAR EVOLUTION

The first car or practical horseless carriage was built by Karl Benz in 1885. It was a carriage with three wheels and a small petrol engine. Benz's car had a top speed of about 13 kilometres (8 miles) per hour. Since then there have been many major changes such as an extra wheel, greater power and air-filled tyres for comfort driving over bumps.

Car designers also need to cover the basics, such as making the car safe to drive. Cars need good brakes and air bags to protect passengers. All cars take a long time to develop from the first idea or **concept**. That's because car makers continually test designs and make improvements.

WHAT iS AN iCONiC CAR?

Iconic cars are the most famous cars. Some are famous because they did something new or did it better than other cars. Some were used by many people. Some are famous because they were beautifully designed.

A car design specification may include how many passengers the car can take and how easy it is to park on crowded city streets.

MODEL T FORD

The Model T or Thin Lizzy was a worldwide hit and was the first popular car.

WORLD OF DESIGN

Constraints

Constraints are limits affecting design. Ford's constraints included cost and ease of use.

In the early 20th century, there were few cars and they were unreliable. Only very rich people could afford to buy them. Designer and **entrepreneur** Henry Ford changed all that when he released his Model T Ford in 1908.

User friendly

The Model T was not only cheap but also user friendly. Ford designed rugged **suspension** springs and the car was high off the ground so that it could carry passengers in comfort on rough roads. He designed a metal cover over the moving parts underneath to stop them from getting damaged. The Model T was also easy to service. With just a few tools it could be turned into anything from a truck to a portable sawmill!

Meeting demand

At first, Ford could not produce enough cars to meet public demand. Ford developed the car **production line** after seeing how watches and sewing machines were made by teams of workers. Each worker stayed in one place and did one job such as bolting on a door. Trolleys carried the part-finished car from one worker to the next. This cut the time for assembling a car from 12 hours to 90 minutes and it allowed the price to fall from US$950 to $260.

CHANGING MARKET

The Model T was so successful that 15 million were sold. Ford saw no reason to change their most successful model. But by the 1920s many drivers wanted something faster and more comfortable. Sales fell, and production ended in 1927.

DUESENBERG J

The Duesenberg J was the most expensive US car of its time. It cost around eight times a doctor's annual salary. For that price, customers were guaranteed extreme luxury.

The 1920s in the United States was a time of poverty for many in rural areas, but some people were getting rich. Cities were growing and people were buying more and more **consumer goods**. Those who made money from this wanted luxury goods such as fast cars. The richest of the rich could afford the iconic Duesenberg J.

Powerful and unique

The engine of the Duesenberg J was twice as powerful as any other. It could quietly speed along at up to 186 kilometres (116 miles) per hour. Customers bought the basic **chassis** and then added the bodywork. They chose the shape, from a town car to a **convertible**. They also chose finishing materials such as rare woods and fine leathers, and, in the 1930s, fittings such as radios!

Customization

Customization means to modify or build something according to individual preference. People buying new cars today can choose colour, fittings, engine power and other **customized** features.

THE BROTHERS DUESENBERG

Fred and Augie Duesenberg moved from Germany to Iowa, USA, towards the end of the 19th century. They started their careers building racing bikes and then moved on to aeroplane engines and racing cars. After the success of the J, they built the even more powerful SJ. Sadly, Fred died when his SJ crashed. Augie failed to keep the Duesenberg car **brand** going on his own.

Volkswagen Beetle

FAST FACTS

Dates: 1938–2003
Designer: Ferdinand Porsche
Special features: air-cooled, rear engine
Top speed: 115 kilometres (71 miles) per hour
Did you know?: In total, over 23 million Beetles were made. The only cars to sell more were the Toyota Corolla and the VW Golf!

DESIGN SPECIFICATION

- Car for family of five costing less than 1,000 German marks

- Able to cruise at 100 kilometres (around 60 miles) per hour in comfort along Germany's smooth *autobahns* (motorways)

- **Fuel economy** of less than 7 litres (1.5 gallons) of fuel per 100 kilometres (62 miles)

- Engine cooled by air not water, and therefore not affected by freezing temperatures

- Easy to repair

The Volkswagen Beetle was first produced in 1938, just as Germany invaded Austria.

On the other side of the Atlantic Ocean, Germany was changing. In 1933, Adolf Hitler became its new leader. He started preparing Germany for war. He created jobs for people and made big improvements to the country, for example by building new roads. Hitler realized there would be demand for a small, cheap car for Germans to get around their growing nation.

Design influences

Hitler paid Ferdinand Porsche to design the new car. Porsche's early shapes were influenced by many other small, smooth-bodied cars around at the time, including the Czech Tatra V570. Hitler sketched a shape for Porsche to base his design on, too.

The Tatra T97 was a Czech car from 1936 designed as a car for the people. Its smooth lines, rear wheel drive and other features provided one of several design inspirations for the VW beetle.

Changes during design

Porsche's original design was improved. A rear window was added and the engine was shifted to the back of the car, rather than the front. This made it cheaper to give the car **rear-wheel drive**. The car was originally called the Volkswagen or People's Car Model 1. It got its nickname "Beetle" due to its short, curved shape.

Wartime production

Porsche set up a brand new factory in Wolfsburg, Germany, to make the Beetle. But during World War II the factory was used to make mostly aeroplane parts and missiles. It also produced military cars based on the Beetle, including the Schwimmwagen – a jeep that turned into a boat!

The rise of VW

At the end of World War II, the Volkswagen factory lay partly in ruins after being bombed by **Allied forces**. However, many machines and parts used to make the car had survived. Allied forces remaining in Germany wanted small cars, so they organized repair of the factory. By the late 1940s, thousands of Beetles were being produced. Volkswagen, or VW, became the name of the car company.

Going global

The Beetle became a global hit during the 1950s and 1960s. The car was popular for its attractive shape, comfort and cheap price. VW **exported** cars worldwide and set up factories in other countries such as Brazil to keep up with demand.

Beetles were used as exciting motorsport cars, too. They appeared in rallies and drag races. Some were even fitted with enormous wheels to become dune buggies that could race across sand.

End of the Beetle

By the mid-1970s there were faster small cars that were also cheaper to run than the Beetle. Sales started to drop. The German VW factory stopped making Beetles and produced the new Golf instead. But Beetles were still made in other parts of the world such as Mexico until 2003.

In 1997 VW released an updated Beetle. It combined the curved shape and fun character of the old one with modern features. In 2012, a redesigned Beetle (above) had a lower profile and looked more like the original Beetle.

Variations on a theme

Volkswagen used the Beetle chassis and engine for other vehicles with other functions. The VW camper had a bus-shaped body for transporting people. The Karmann Ghia had a low, sporty body for a faster drive than the Beetle.

THE JEEP

FAST FACTS

Type of car: Military vehicle
Produced by: Bantam
First produced: 1940

Many people drive jeeps today, but they were first designed as World War II military vehicles. It was a general purpose car for shifting troops and weapons short distances. When soldiers shortened its name to GP and said it quickly, it sounded like "jeep"! The jeep was designed to be tough enough to travel over rough land and strong enough to have mounted machine guns. But it was also light enough to be lifted by four men or be lifted by a plane and parachuted into battle fields.

MEDAL WINNERS

Jeeps were so popular among troops during World War II, that one jeep called "Old Faithful" was even given a Purple Heart (a US medal awarded to those killed or injured during service) and sent home for surviving two beach landings!

Over 600,000 jeeps were built. Soldiers loved them. The jeep did everything and went everywhere. It often carried twice what it was designed for and still kept going.

RIVAL FIRMS

In June 1940 car manufacturer Bantam won the **commission** to design and build the first jeeps for the US Army. The firm worked hard and fast to meet the Army's specifications. But when two rival companies, Willys and Ford, came up with their own designs, the US government decided upon a standard design based on all three jeeps. The government gave the contract to make the jeeps to Willys and Ford. Bantam was left to make trailers to be used with the jeeps.

Commission

A commission is a request to design or make something.

Modern jeeps, like the originals, are designed to be able to climb steep slopes and even cross shallow streams.

MERCEDES 300SL

FAST FACTS

Type of car: Sports car
Produced by: Mercedes Benz
First produced: 1952 (as a racing car); 1954 (as a luxury sports car)

After World War II, there was more interest in small, personal cars which could be driven for fun as well as for travel. The Mercedes 300SL was originally designed as a racing car. To cut down on **drag**, or **air resistance**, the Mercedes 300SL was wide and deep at the bottom but narrower higher up. This meant the sills didn't have room for door hinges. Designer Rudy Uhlenhaut and his team put the hinges on the roof. The doors opened upwards, like the flapping wings of a bird!

GYMNASTIC DRIVER!

On the first **prototypes** (early versions), the door was tiny and the only way for a driver sitting inside the car to get out of it was to remove the steering wheel first and then climb up and out!

When both doors are open it is obvious how the Mercedes 300SL got its nickname "Gull Wing". In 1999 this iconic ride was voted "Sports car of the century"!

Going public

At first, the German Daimler-Benz company had no plans to produce the 300SL for the public, but Maximilian ("Maxi") Hoffman had other ideas. Maxi **imported** Mercedes-Benz cars into the United States. He argued long and hard to persuade the company to make a sports car for his rich buyers. The 300SL was unveiled in New York in 1954 at the United States' most important car show and crowds were wowed by a race that showcased its speed and style.

FAST AND COMFORTABLE

The 300SL was popular among film stars and the rich and famous not only for its smooth, sleek look and cool, racing car image, but also because it was a fast and comfortable car.

The 300SL had a luxurious leather interior.

CITROËN DS

At the Paris Motor Show in 1955, a new luxury French car was unveiled. The Citroën DS had a smoothly curved design that made it look like something from the future. It caused quite a stir among visitors and sold 750 in the first 45 minutes. There were 12,000 orders for the design in the first 24 hours!

This open-top cabriolet version of the Citroën DS went on display at the 1960 Paris Motor Show.

The DS design evolved from first to final ideas. But all had a smooth, **streamlined** shape with covered back wheels to make it drive at speed using less power.

Automotive engineer

Person who designs, develops and tests motor vehicles and improves parts such as engines and shape to make cars more powerful or have better fuel economy.

SKID SAVER

In 1962 French President Charles de Gaulle was travelling in a DS when some people fired guns at it. The presidential car had bullet-proof glass fitted but bullets punctured all of the tyres. Thankfully, the hydraulic suspension stopped the car from losing control and skidding.

Innovation

Flaminio Bertoni was the automotive engineer responsible for the modern appearance of the Citroën DS. He used man-made materials such as plastic for the roof and curved dashboard. Such materials were unusual in cars at that time. But the design hid many **innovative** technical features, too. One of these was the **hydraulic system**. This network of oil-filled tubes was used to power the steering, gear change and for suspension. The suspension could be adjusted to make driving along France's bumpy roads a smooth experience.

Flaminio Bertoni

FAST FACTS

Dates: 1903–1964
From: Italy
Company: Citroën
Most iconic designs: Traction Avant, 2CV, DS
Did you know? Bertoni was also an **architect**.
He designed low-cost housing for St Louis, USA.

Bertoni was born in northern Italy and loved drawing and sculpting. He became a car designer by accident after his father's death because he needed to leave art college and earn money to help his family. Bertoni got a job as an **apprentice** at a local car maker. He became head designer and then set up his own design studio while continuing as an artist and sculptor.

Bertoni was a skilled sculptor. He designed the flowing shape of the Traction Avant (shown above) by shaping it in plasticine without drawing it first.

To Citroën

Bertoni fell in love with a woman of whom his family disapproved. The couple married and moved to Paris, France, to live. Bertoni got a job at the innovative car maker Citroën. There he worked closely with mechanical engineer André Lefebvrè on their new front-wheel drive car, the Traction Avant. Bertoni and Lefebvrè went on to work together on the 2CV and DS.

2CV

Bertoni's other iconic car was the 2CV. The design brief was for a cheap, small car that France's large rural population could use to get around and transport goods. Citroën requested a car with suspension capable of driving over a ploughed field carrying eggs without them breaking. They also wanted a roof that could open up to carry large objects. The 2CV appeared in 1948 and remained in production until 1990.

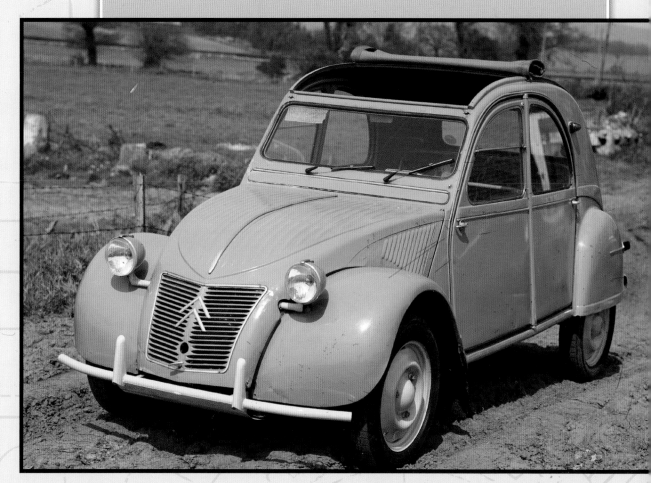

Bertoni's 2CV was first designed to transport four farmers and 50 kilograms (110 pounds) of goods at 60 kilometres (37 miles) per hour to market! But its fun design proved popular for town and city drivers too.

1959 CADILLAC

WORLD OF DESIGN

Design influence

Design influence is the way that what is happening in the wider world can influence designs in fashion, art, transport and other areas.

Design is often influenced by other things going on in the world. During the late 1950s, people the world over were fascinated by the new modern jet aeroplanes. There was fierce competition between Russia and the United States to be the first country to get a man into space. This led to an interest in rocket-type car designs, especially in the United States. The Cadillac from 1959 was one of the most iconic.

The 1959 Cadillac Coupe de Ville weighed nearly 2.5 tonnes and was over 2 metres (6 $\frac{1}{2}$ feet) wide but is most famous for its extreme tail fins!

The Cadillac had several features to create a jet or rocket-like appearance. Its flowing design reminded people of rocket shapes. It had tall, pointed **tail fins**, inspired by the fins that stick up from the end of a fighter plane's tail to help keep a plane steady as it flies in the air. The Cadillac also had large, bullet-shaped brake lights and was covered in lots of shiny, silver chrome to give it an exciting, space-age feel.

FINISHING WITH FINS

Many cars copied the Cadillac tail fins and tail fins grew in popularity for about a decade. People became bored with them after the United States lost the early space race in 1961, when Russia sent the first man into space.

Chrysler also designed cars with distinctive tail fins.

THE MINI

On the other side of the Atlantic in the United Kingdom, fuel was in short supply and being **rationed** (shared out). People in the United Kingdom bought fewer new cars, but German **bubblecars** were very popular. They had high fuel economy. Then in 1959, the British Motor Corporation introduced their own small car – the Mini. It was a great success.

The Mini was known as the world's most advanced family car, yet it cost just under £500. It proved to be very popular and sold over 1 million within six years. A new design of the Mini is still in production today.

Small car

The Mini was designed by Sir Alec Issigonis. His design specification was to make a small car that was less than 3 metres (10 feet) long of which 1.8 metres (6 feet) was space for four passengers. With its small size and light weight the Mini could travel at over 6.5 litres of fuel per 100 kilometres (40 miles per gallon).

LESS OIL

In the mid-1950s, there was conflict between Egypt and the UK (and other countries) over the Suez Canal. This canal was a vital shipping route from Africa to Asia. In protest, some oil-rich countries in the Middle East stopped exporting oil to the UK. This decreased supply of oil meant that cars like the Mini, which used less fuel, became popular.

Space-saving features

Issigonis used several space-saving features:

- Small wheels, which needed smaller arches, taking up less interior space
- Engine mounted sideways rather than lengthways under the bonnet
- Front-wheel drive – in most cars the engine turned the rear wheels using a bulky drive shaft
- Rubber shock absorbers rather than bulky metal springs to absorb bumps on the road
- Sliding windows – the gear to wind windows took up space inside the door

E-TYPE JAGUAR

FAST FACTS

Type of car: Sports car
Produced by: Jaguar Cars
First produced: 1961

In 1961, Jaguar released a car that even today is widely thought of as one of the most beautiful cars ever built. However, the smooth shape of the E-type was not designed just to turn heads, but to move smoothly and quickly.

This E-type Jaguar has a covered passenger compartment. Some people thought it looked a little like an aeroplane without wings!

Aeroplanes to cars

The E-type designer was an aeroplane engineer called Malcolm Sayer. Sayer used complex maths calculations to find the best curves for the new car just as he had for wings and aeroplane bodies. His aim was to reduce drag. A smooth, pointed streamlined shape has less drag than a rougher, flat shape. With less drag a vehicle has better fuel economy.

Light and fast

The E-type was developed from one of the prize-winning racing cars that Sayer created. It had a small, powerful engine and lightweight aluminium body to reduce weight. The E-type had a top speed of 240 kilometres (150 miles) per hour. It could accelerate from 0 to 100 kilometres (0 to 60 miles) per hour in 7 seconds.

DRAG TESTING

Sayer tested drag on early versions, or prototypes, of the E-type by taping tufts of wool to the outside. He then drove alongside the speeding car to see how the wool was flattened by air flowing over its surface! If there was too little flattening, he remodelled the shape to make air flow faster.

Malcolm Sayer designed many sleek, **aerodynamic** cars for Jaguar during the 1950s and 60s, such as this C-type.

LOTUS 72

At the time when the E-type Jaguar came out, the fastest cars in the world were not on the road but those that took part in Formula 1 (F1) Grand Prix races on tracks in 13 different countries. One of the most iconic F1 designs was the Lotus 72 from 1970.

The new nose combined with other changes such as a large wing made the Lotus 72 a race-winning car.

DESIGN FOR SPEED

A road car needs to be comfortable for several passengers, but racing cars are all about speed for one driver. Design teams have achieved faster speeds in racing cars by putting in better engines and adding rear wings to reduce drag. They have helped cars keep better control when speeding around corners by keeping weight close to the road, using airflow to pull the car towards the track, and by adding thicker tyres and even extra wheels!

New shape

Before the Lotus 72, F1 cars had a hole at the front, like road cars, to take air to the engine. The air burns fuel to power the car and helps cool the engine. The trouble is that the intake causes drag. Designer Colin Chapman designed the 72 with a wedge-shaped front and no hole. The shape forced air to flow around into holes at the sides leading to the engine. This change of shape alone let the Lotus 72 go 14 kilometres (8.7 miles) per hour faster than an earlier Lotus with exactly the same engine but with a hole at the front.

GRAND PRIX WINNER

The Lotus 72 almost immediately started to win Grand Prix races. In 1970, Jochen Rindt won four in a row, but sadly had a fatal crash when practising for a race. No other driver matched his points so Rindt was declared world champion after his death. Rindt was replaced by the Brazilian driver Emerson Fittipaldi, who won the US Grand Prix in 1970 and went on to be world champion in 1972 and 1973 driving the Lotus 72. In total the car won 20 out of 75 races before its retirement in 1975, taking 5th place in the US Grand Prix. By then the 72 could not compete with the better F1 cars made by Ferrari and Brabham.

AUDI QUATTRO

The Audi Quattro is a chunky, heavy looking car that lacks the obvious design appeal of, say, the Citroen DS or E-type Jaguar. But this 1980 car achieves its iconic status because of its fantastic road-gripping performance.

The Quattro looked very "boxy" and chunky but drivers loved the way it handled.

Snow mobile

In the late 1970s, Audi engineers witnessed tests of a four wheel drive (4WD) off-roader developed by Volkswagen for the military and forest workers. It barely slipped on snowy roads. This spurred the Audi team to develop a 4WD road car. It coped well on steep, snowy hills but the wife of an Audi director who borrowed the prototype one weekend complained. She said the car "hopped" when cornering and was difficult to park. Designers adjusted the 4WD system so that it worked perfectly. The system was driven by a **turbocharged** engine that adjusted itself via computer to work powerfully at all times.

Hand built

Quattros were expensive because of the high-specification parts inside but also because they were handmade. Each car took seven days to build and was tested more thoroughly before sale than any other car. For example, a Quattro was tested for how waterproof it was by having water sprayed on it for 10 minutes. Most cars were tested for just 30 seconds.

THE FiRST 4WD CAR

The Jensen Interceptor was the first high-performance 4WD car. Apart from being expensive it had a major design flaw. The inside was set up so that a driver could only be on the right for driving on the left side of the road. Therefore, the Interceptor could not be sold in countries where people drove on the right!

Designer in focus

Martin Smith

FAST FACTS

Dates: Born 1949
From: UK
Companies: Porsche, Audi, Opel/Vauxhall, Ford
Most iconic designs: 911 Turbo, Quattro, Zafira, Astra, Mondeo, Fiesta...
Did you know? Smith designed Luke Skywalker's Landspeeder for the film *Star Wars!*

Martin Smith designed the Audi Quattro in his early thirties. He wanted to be a car designer from a young age but was advised by Alec Issigonis to study engineering first. After completing an engineering degree in the United Kingdom, Smith studied vehicle design and got his first job with Porsche in Germany.

A working life

Then he moved on to Audi for 20 years, followed by 7 years at Opel/Vauxhall and 10 as Executive Design Director at Ford. In these periods he designed the Audi 80, 100 and Quattro, and the multi-person Vauxhall Zafira. He also redesigned and increased sales of many long-standing brands such as the Astra, Mondeo and Fiesta.

Martin Smith's engineering background has helped him create practical designs for cars.

Energy in motion

At Ford, Smith created a new "kinetic design" style. In this he used bold lines, shapes and finishes to represent energy in motion. For example, his redesigned Fiesta had stretched headlights, a tapering moulded line down its side and a large front grille tapering backwards at its corners. These design elements made it look like the Fiesta was moving even when it was standing still.

Luke Skywalker's Landspeeder was one of Martin Smith's many and varied vehicle designs. It appeared in Stars Wars films from 1977. The body shape was fitted over a smaller car so that it looked as if the Landspeeder was floating.

TOYOTA PRIUS

As people became more concerned about rising fuel prices and the **pollution** caused by burning petrol to power cars, there was a need for a new kind of car. Toyota released its four-passenger Prius hybrid in 1997. It was the first car with a fuel-saving, less-polluting **hybrid engine** to sell in large numbers. Hybrid means combining two different things. A hybrid car combines a petrol engine with an electric motor. The Prius has a distinctive wedge shape, which helps to improve the car's aerodynamics and reduce drag.

How hybrids work

- Hybrid cars use batteries to supply power to a small electric motor that drives the car in cities and on slower roads.
- They use petrol engines to drive the car at high speeds on motorways, when petrol engines use fuel more efficiently, and to power the car if the battery runs out.
- The petrol engine is also used to recharge the motor's battery.
- When the car is going downhill or braking, the wheels turn because of the car's **momentum** to power the electric motor and recharge the batteries.
- When more power is needed, the petrol engine and the electric motor can even work together!

A Battery recharge plug
B Fuel tank
C Electric battery pack
D Electric motor
E Engine

WEDGE DESIGN

Part of the appeal of the Prius was its distinctive, triangular wedge shape, but designers Katsuhiko Inatomi and Norio Oseki created the wedge shape for more than looks alone. More importantly, this shape helps to improve the car's aerodynamics and reduce drag. This improves the car's fuel economy.

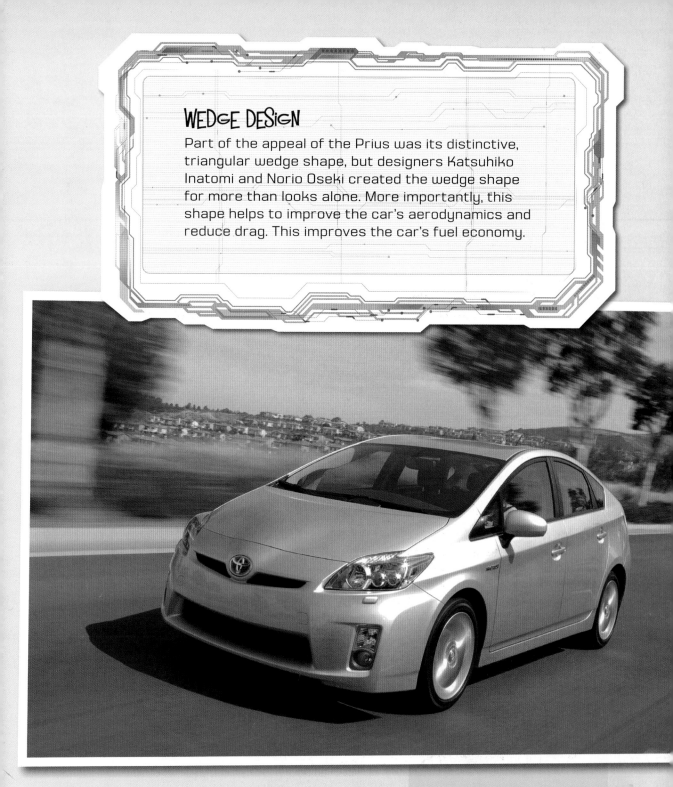

Another benefit of hybrid cars is that when they are running on their electric motor they are very quiet.

Smart Car

FAST FACTS

Date: 1998–present
Designer: Johann Tomforde
Special features: metal Tridion cell, plastic body panels
Top speed: up to 150 kilometres (96 miles) per hour
Fuel economy: up to 130 kilometres (85 miles) per gallon
Did you know? Over 1.5 million Smart Cars have been sold worldwide

The Smart Car is an iconic micro car that first appeared in 1998. But work on designing this vehicle began in 1972. Then there was a global oil crisis when car fuel was in short supply.

Planning for the future

The Mercedes Benz car company realized there would be demand around the year 2000 and beyond for a tiny car that used little fuel. The company designed the car to be easy to park and used in busy city streets. It also caused very little pollution as it only needed slow top speeds.

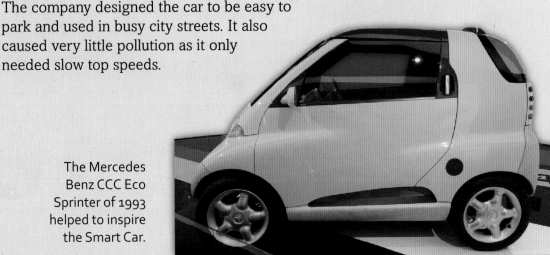

The Mercedes Benz CCC Eco Sprinter of 1993 helped to inspire the Smart Car.

Smart Fortwo coupe
269.5 cm (106.1 inches) long

Mini Cooper coupe
370 cm (145.6 inches) long

Toyota Camry saloon
480.5 cm (189.2 inches) long

Smart Fortwo coupe
156 cm (61.4 inches) wide

Hummer H2 SUV 517 cm (203.5 inches) long

3 Smart Car parking spaces = 1 Hummer parking space

Development

Designer Johann Tomforde created several prototypes for a micro car. These included the electric NAFA car, which was never produced due to safety concerns, and the Mercedes City Car, which was taller, safer and more powerful. By 1993, Tomforde had the basic designs for the Mercedes City Car ready. But the car did not go into production until Nicolas Hayek became involved.

DESIGN SPECIFICATION

- Short length – 2.5 metres (7 feet) maximum length making it easy to manoeuvre and to park. It can even be parked at right angles to the kerb when space is tight!

- Space for two people and luggage

- Safe to drive: many small cars at the time were not very strong

- Economical electric or hybrid engine

Watches to cars

Rather like Henry Ford, Hayek wanted to make cars in the same way as watches! Hayek had invented Swatch watches and developed them into a global brand. They were cheap to make because they needed fewer parts than traditional watches. They could be easily customized with lots of colorful parts. Mercedes collaborated with Swatch and the Smart Car brand was born.

Smart release

The first Smart Cars had tiny gasoline and diesel engines, which had the lowest **emissions** of any car engines. The first electric engines appeared around 10 years later, once they had greater reliability and battery storage. Models varied from the basic ForTwo to convertibles. Later Smart Cars included the larger ForFour (for four passengers) and faster Roadster.

WORLD OF DESIGN

Materials technologist

Person who works with materials such as metals, plastics, rubbers and ceramics. They use their expert knowledge to help engineers use the best materials for their designs.

Safe and attractive materials

All Smart Cars are built around a tough, steel cage called a Tridion cell that protects passengers in the event of crashes. Recyclable plastic panels are attached on top. This material has advantages over metal as it is light, does not rust, and is bump and scratch-resistant. Also, it allows for easy customization of the color and style of a customer's Smart Car.

Smart Cars have an impressive safety history, making them both a pleasant and safe drive.

SMARTVILLE

Most Smart Cars are made in a purpose-built factory in eastern France called Smartville. It has a production line designed to reduce its environmental impact. For example, it uses powder paint rather than paint mixed with harmful chemicals to paint the car parts. It recycles heat lost from machines for warming the factory and water. It also employs nearby small companies to make the parts, which avoids the need to transport parts over long distances.

BUGATTI VEYRON

FAST FACTS

Type of car: Supercar
Produced by: Bugatti Automobiles
First produced: 2005

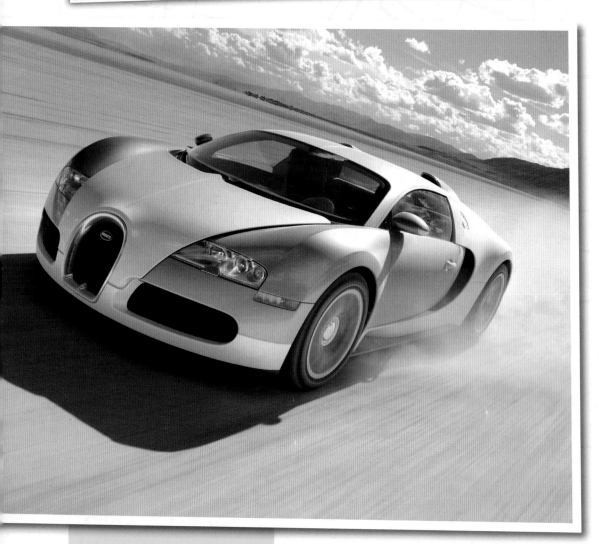

The Bugatti Veyron was named after Pierre Veyron, Bugatti's winner of the Le Mans race in 1939.

A need for speed

The Bugatti Veyron is one of the fastest cars on Earth that is allowed to drive on main roads. It can reach speeds of more than 400 kilometers (250 miles) per hour and accelerate to 100 kilometers (60 miles) per hour in under 2.5 seconds. Its engine is so large that it is fixed halfway along the car for balance! The Veyron's high speed capability combined with its classic styling – large radiator, two-tone coloring and luxurious leather interior – make this car an icon of the modern age.

Bugatti reborn

The Bugatti car company was no longer working in 1998 when the Volkswagen Group purchased the rights to use and revive the Bugatti brand. VW wanted to build a luxury car that was faster than any other and what better name to use than Bugatti, which was world-famous for luxury and race cars. VW presented the first Bugatti Veyron at the Tokyo Motor Show in 1999. From 2001 they made about 80 a year, for super-rich customers who usually collected the cars from the factory in Alsace, France, themselves!

BRAKE POWER

In order to be safe, a fast car like the Veyron needs to be able to stop quickly. The Veyron has ceramic brakes rather like F1 cars, and a **spoiler** at the back that can rise up to increase drag and help to slow the car down. The Veyron can stop from travelling at 100 kilometres (62 miles) per hour in under 3 seconds and from its top speed in 10 seconds – although the distance covered in this time is half a kilometre ($\frac{1}{3}$ mile)!

THE FUTURE OF CAR DESIGN

We have seen many iconic cars from the past and present, but what of the future? What factors and limitations will shape car designs in the future and what might they look like?

NEW MARKETS

New cars are also being designed for rapidly **developing countries** where many people are only now able to afford them, such as India and China. The Nano Tato is a very cheap, very small car designed for city driving in India. By contrast, the Buick Lacrosse is designed for the very wealthy in China who have chauffeurs, so the focus is on roomy, luxurious back seats!

Better for the environment

The main emphasis for car designers now is on creating cars that cause less damage to the environment. The Tesla Model S is a completely electric car that can accelerate from 0 to 100 kilometres (0 to 60 miles) per hour in 5.4 seconds and creates zero emissions on the road. You can plug it in at home overnight, but until there are more recharging stations, longer journeys take some planning.

The Tesla S looks sleek and modern, makes no noise and can be seen topping up its batteries at a charging station near you!

The Buick Envision that premiered in Beijing in 2014 is a luxury SUV. Its front grille, shiny chrome and dynamic styling were designed for the growing group of young, rich Chinese people.

Air car

A car that runs on air sounds like it belongs in a sci-fi film, but people might be driving them sooner than you think. In 2014, Peugeot designed a new type of hybrid car, the Tata Nano, which combines a motor that runs on compressed (squashed) air with a petrol engine.

FORMULA E

There is a new kind of motor racing called Formula E. It is for electric racing cars only. The races happen in city centres and have a festival atmosphere with music and celebrities. The races could help make electric cars popular in the future.

TIMELINE

1769 The first steam-powered road vehicle is invented to move heavy cannons, very slowly

1885 Karl Benz invents the first practical horseless carriage or car with three wheels and a petrol engine

1908 Henry Ford designs the cheap, dependable Model T Ford

1928 The luxurious Duesenberg J is released. It can be customized to the tastes of the super-rich.

1938 The Beetle, commissioned by Adolf Hitler in Germany, goes into production briefly in 1938 and then from 1945 to 2003.

1940 Willys jeep is created for the US Army for wartime use. It is a tough, small, light, all-purpose 4WD vehicle used widely ever since.

1948 French car company Citroën releases the 2CV. This fun but practical car is designed primarily for the large farming population to drive its goods from field to market.

1954 The Mercedes 300SL small sports car is unveiled with its unusual Gull Wing doors

1955 The futuristic Citroën DS is presented for the first time at the Paris Motor Show. Its design is later hailed as one of the most beautiful ever.

1959 The Cadillac, like many US cars of this time, has large "space rocket" fins on its rear end

1959 Sir Alec Issigonis designs the Mini. Its small but spacious design is popular at a time when people are worried about oil supplies.

1961 The E-type Jaguar goes on sale. This beautiful, streamlined sports car is designed by ex-aeronautical engineer Malcolm Sayer.

1970 The first wedge-fronted F1 car – the Lotus 72 – starts to race. It wins 20 Grand Prix races, two drivers championships and three constructors championships.

1980 The hand-made Audi Quattro 4WD saloon car goes on sale. Its chunky design represents its hidden power.

1997 The Toyota Prius is the world's first popular hybrid engine car

1998 Smart Cars go on sale. These safe micro city cars are highly economical and easy to manoeuvre through congested city streets.

1999 The luxury supercar Bugatti Veyron is the fastest street-legal car on Earth

2007 Honda creates the first hydrogen car ready for production

2012 The Tesla S all-electric sports car is released to wide acclaim. It can accelerate as fast as a normal car but is as environmentally friendly as a Smart Car.

GLOSSARY

aerodynamic describes how well something moves through the air

air resistance force of air that slows down a car or plane

Allied forces countries that fought together against Germany in WWI and WWII

apprentice person who is learning a skill while working for an employer

architect person who designs buildings

brand type of product made by a company under a particular name

bubblecar small car with a clear, curved roof and often three wheels

chassis frame around which a vehicle such as a car is built

commission ask someone to create or produce something, such as a new car design

concept idea, invention or plan

constraint restriction or limitation

consumer goods things people buy, such as TVs and washing machines

convertible car with a roof that can be taken off or folded down

customize make or change something to please the owner or buyer

design influence thing that persuades a designer to design items in a certain way

developing country country that is growing richer

drag another word for *air resistance* (see above)

emissions gases released into the air

entrepreneur person who makes money by starting and running new businesses

export send and sell goods to another country

fuel economy describes how far a car can travel on a certain amount of fuel

hybrid engine engine that combines a petrol engine with another type of engine, such as an electric motor

hydraulic system machine that works by using the force created by pushing a liquid through pipes

import bring in and buy goods from another country

innovative describes a new, original idea or way of doing something

momentum tendency of an object to keep moving in the same direction

pollution when air, water, and other parts of the environment are contaminated or made dirty by waste, chemicals and other harmful substances

production line line of workers and machines in a factory working on different stages of the same product

prototype first version of a design, which is usually improved upon in later designs

ration limit the amount of something someone can have

rear-wheel drive system that provides power to the rear (back) wheels of a vehicle

specification detailed description of how a design or something else should be done

spoiler part that is raised up on the back of a car or plane to increase its air resistance

streamlined shaped to reduce air resistance and move through the air easily and quickly

suspension system of springs and shock absorbers supporting a vehicle on its wheels, which makes it more comfortable to drive and ride in

tail fin part that sticks up at the end of a vehicle. The fin helps to keep it steady when it moves or is there for decoration.

turbocharged when a vehicle is fitted with a device that makes it faster and more powerful

FIND OUT MORE

Books

Car Science, Richard Hammond (Dorling Kindersley, 2011)

Cars (Design and Engineering), Ian Graham (Raintree, 2014)

How Cars Work, Nick Arnold (Templar, 2012)

Know it All: Cars, Andrew Langley (Franklin Watts, 2014)

Websites

www.f1scarlet.com/evolution_f1car.html
See how the designs of F1 cars have changed over time by looking at the pictures on this website.

formula1.ferrari.com/history
Find out about the development of Ferrari race cars from this website.

www.pininfarina.it/en/services/automotive_design
Pininfarina is one of the world's most famous car design studios. Visit their website and click on "design stories" before browsing their automotive designs by decade. For a summary of the company's history and collaborations with different car makers, click on "company/history".

www.toyota.co.jp/en/kids/car/index.html
Learn about all the steps involved in planning, designing, testing and producing cars. This site includes some fascinating illustrations and videos of each step.

Ideas for research

If you would like to be a car designer one day, then visit:
www.cardesignnews.com/site/home/display/store4/item50380
to see what skills you might need to develop and which colleges run courses.

Find out as much as you can about product design; there are some fascinating interviews with designers and studies of iconic designs at:
www.designmuseum.org/design.

Places to visit

Beaulieu National Motor Museum
John Montagu Building, Beaulieu
Brockenhurst, Hampshire SO42 7ZN
Tel: 01590 612345
Email: info@beaulieu.co.uk
Website: www.beaulieu.co.uk
This museum has a collection of cars telling the history
of motoring modern rally cars and F1 Grand
Prix machines.

Design Museum
28 Shad Thames, London SE1 2YD
Tel: 020 7940 8783
Email: tickets@designmuseum.org
Website: www.designmuseum.org
This museum covers product, industrial, graphic,
fashion and architectural design.

Haynes International Motor Museum
Sparkford, Yeovil, Somerset BA22 7LH
Tel: 01963 440 804
Email: museum@haynesmotormuseum.co.uk
Website: www.haynesmotormuseum.com
This museum has the UK's largest exhibition of the greatest
vehicles from around the world with over 400 cars and bikes.

The Bubblecar Museum
Clover Farm, Main Road, Langrick
Boston, Linconshire PE22 7AW
Tel: 01205 280037
Email: contact form on website
Website: www.bubblecarmuseum.co.uk
At this museum you can see 50 bubblecars and even take
a ride in one!

INDEX

acceleration 27, 41, 42
aerodynamics 27, 34, 35
air bags 5
Audi Quattro 30–31, 32
automotive engineers 19

Bantam 14, 15
batteries 34, 38, 42
Benz, Karl 4
Bertoni, Flaminio 19, 20–21
brakes 5, 41
British Motor Company 24
bubblecars 24
Bugatti Veyron 40–41
Buick Envision 43
Buick Lacrosse 42

Cadillac 22–23
campers 13
Chapman, Colin 29
Citroen 18–21
Citroën 2CV 20, 21
Citroën DS 18–19
commissions 15
compressed air 43
customization 9, 38

design influence 11, 22
design specification 4, 5,
    10, 25, 37
diesel engines 38
drag 16, 27, 28, 29, 34, 35, 41
Duesenberg, Fred and Augie
    9
Duesenberg J 8–9
dune buggies 12

E-Type Jaguar 26–27
electric motors 34, 35,
    37, 38, 42, 43

first car 4
Ford, Henry 6, 7, 38
Ford Fiesta 33

Formula 1 cars 28–29
Formula E cars 43
four-wheel drive (4WD) 31
front-wheel drive 20, 25
fuel economy 10, 19, 24,
    25, 27, 35, 36
future car design 42–43

General Motors 22
Gull Wing see Mercedes
    300SL

hand built cars 31
Hayek, Nicolas 37–38
Hoffman, Maximilian 17
hybrid cars 34–35, 43
hydraulic suspension 19

iconic cars 4, 5
Inatomi, Katsuhiko 35
Issigonis, Sir Alec 25, 32

Jaguar Cars 26–27
Jeep 14–15
Jensen Interceptor 31

Karmann Ghia 13
"kinetic design" style 33

Landspeeder 32, 33
Lefebvre, André 20
Lotus 72 28–29

materials technologists 38
Mercedes 300SL 16–17
Mercedes Benz 16–17, 36, 38
Mini 24–25
Model T Ford 6–7

oil crises 25, 36
Oseki, Norio 35

parking 5, 31, 36, 37
petrol engines 4, 34, 38, 43

Peugeot 43
pollution 34, 36
Porsche, Ferdinand 10, 11
production lines 7
prototypes 16, 27, 31, 37

racing cars 16, 17, 27, 28–29,
    43
rally cars 30–31
rear-wheel drive 11, 25
rocket-type car designs
    22–23

Sayer, Malcolm 27
shock absorbers 25
Smart cars 36–39
Smith, Martin 32–33
space-saving features 25
speeds 4, 9, 10, 21, 27, 36, 41
sports cars 16–17
supercars 40–41
suspension 7, 19, 21
SUVs 4, 37, 43

tail fins 22, 23
Tata Nano 42, 43
Tatra V570 11
Tesla S 42
Tomforde, Johan 36, 37
Toyota Prius 34–35
Traction Avant 20
Tridion cell 38
turbocharged engines 31
tyres 4, 19, 28

Uhlenhaut, Rudy 16

Volkswagen Beetle 10–13